Photography by:
Günter Ziesler, Clem Haagner, ARDEA,
Ian Beames, Arthus Bertrand, Hugo van Lawick,
D. Parer and E. Parer-Cook.

GIRAFFE FAMILY
Jane Goodall

A MADISON MINI BOOK

Published by Madison Marketing Limited.
Madison Marketing Limited holds the exclusive
license to this edition.
Copyright © 1991 by Neugebauer Rights & Licenses AG., Zurich.
Text copyright © 1991 by Jane Goodall.
All rights reserved.
ISBN 1-55066-015-2

Printed in Canada

Printed on recycled paper

GIRAFFE FAMILY

Jane Goodall
ANIMAL SERIES

Photographs selected by
Michael Neugebauer

Madison Marketing Limited

The first time I saw George close up I couldn't believe how tall he was – at least 20 feet high! Everything about him is long. He looks down at you from huge dark eyes fringed with beautiful long eyelashes. When he feeds he uses his long blue-black tongue to pull leaves from high branches. He can eat sharp thorny twigs because the inside of his mouth is quite hard and horny.

George likes to hang about near our camp on the Serengeti. Sometimes I follow him as he walks across the African plains, swinging along on his six-foot-high legs. I always love to watch him run. He seems to glide across the ground in slow motion. Really, though, he's going as fast as a horse. He covers about 15 feet with each stride.

George sometimes feeds by himself and sometimes near other giraffes.

One day we come upon a tiny newborn baby. He is lying on the ground and his mother is licking him dry. I name him Friday, for the day he is born.

It takes Friday about half an hour to stand up. Since giraffes have such long legs it's very difficult for them. At last Friday manages to get all four legs under him. But as soon as he tries to take a step he falls. Then he tries again. And falls again. After seven tries he manages to reach his mother's flank. He nuzzles there, finds a nipple, and starts to suckle. Friday looks very small beside his mother, Masie. In fact, he is already six feet tall!

Nearby is a group of six giraffes – one male, two females with calves, and one youngster of about a year. Masie and Friday move towards them. They all stare, but only the yearling approaches. He looks at the new baby, but he doesn't touch him. When Masie begins to feed, Friday lies down to rest. One of the other young ones, about six months old, is suckling. In another few weeks he'll be weaned from his mother's milk and fending for himself.

This year it is very dry. The plains are hot and dusty and most of the water holes have dried out. A lot of giraffes and other animals stay near our camp by the river, so I'm able to see little Friday quite often. He grows very quickly – about half an inch a day for the first few days! After that he slows down a bit. Masie is very loving while he is small and often nuzzles him and caresses him with her tongue.

Friday is very inquisitive. He watches the other animals who often feed near the giraffes – the zebras and wart hogs and ostriches. Sometimes he comes near my car and peers inside with his big soft eyes. His mother never tries to stop him.

Some days Masie feeds near a group of males. Friday is always fascinated when two of the younger males have friendly "pushing matches." They stand side by side and press the upper part of their necks together, pushing hard. This is the way they find out who is stronger. One day I see two of them having a real fight. They swing their necks towards each other and smash into each other with their heads. But as far as I can tell, no one gets hurt. In the end one moves away, defeated.

One day I follow Masie and Friday when they go to a drinking place along the river. They pass some lions who just go on drowsing. Lions do hunt giraffes, but not often. Friday would make a nice meal, but his mother is too close. An adult giraffe has a very powerful kick that can hurt a lion badly.

Even so, Masie is anxious as she begins to drink. She has to spread her front legs wide apart in order to reach the water. It looks very awkward. A lion could creep up and seize her baby. Every few minutes Masie stands up and looks all around. When she is sure that all is safe, she straddles her legs again and continues to drink.

Friday is two months old when the first rains come. Most of the reachable leaves on the trees near the river have been nibbled away, and many of the giraffes wander off in search of new feeding places. By this time Friday is steady on his long legs. He can even run faster than his mother.

One evening Masie and Friday start moving out across the plains. They are going towards the distant hills where the sun is setting. Soon they are far away, just two dark shapes against the red African sky. I know that they, too, are headed for new feeding grounds.

I'm feeling sad as I drive back to camp. It seems that all the giraffes have moved away for a while. But then I see a tall shape moving under one of the trees. It's George.

$\mathcal{J}$ANE GOODALL has shared her important discoveries and her love of animals with millions of people around the world through books, films and lectures. She has founded ongoing research and educational institutes on two continents, and is one of the world's most acclaimed naturalists.

The Jane Goodall Institute for Wildlife
Research, Education and Conservation
P.O. Box 41720, Tucson, AZ 85717 U.S.A.

The Jane Goodall Institute — Canada
P.O. Box 3125, Station "C"
Ottawa, Ontario K1Y 4J4 Canada

The Jane Goodall Institute — U.K.
15 Clarendon Park
Lymington, Hants SO41 8AX United Kingdom